Toronto-Vancouver TransCanadian Sketchbook

5/12 - 8/12/2006 -

First published in English in Canada in 2009 by
McArthur & Company
322 King Street West, Suite 402
Toronto, Ontario
M5V 1J2
www.mcarthur-co.com

First published in French by Actes Sud in 2009 as *Carnet Transcanadien*

Library and Archives Canada Cataloguing in Publication

Barrot, Olivier
TransCanadian sketchbook / written by Olivier Barrot ; illustrated by Alain Bouldouyre ; translated by Dawn M. Cornelio.

Translation of: Carnet transcanadien
ISBN 978-1-55278-811-0

    1. Barrot, Olivier--Travel--Canada. 2. Bouldouyre, Alain--Travel--Canada. _3. Railroad travel--Canada. 4. Canada--In art. 5. Canada--Description and travel. 6. VIA Rail Canada. I. Bouldouyre, Alain II. Cornelio, Dawn M. III. Title.

FC75.B373 2009   917.104'7   C2009-904010-7

The publisher would like to acknowledge the financial support of the Government of Canada through the Book Publishing Industry Development Program (BPIDP) and the Canada Council for our publishing activities. The publisher further wishes to acknowledge the financial support of the Ontario Arts Council and the OMDC for our publishing program.

Design and composition by Cécile Barroul, Arles
Photogravure by Terre neuve, Arles
Photographs and illustrations by Alain Bouldouyre
Printed in Canada by Friesens

10 9 8 7 6 5 4 3 2 1

TransCanadian Sketchbook

Toronto–Vancouver on board *The Canadian*

TEXT
OLIVIER BARROT

DRAWINGS AND PHOTOS
ALAIN BOULDOUYRE

TRANSLATION
DAWN M. CORNELIO

McArthur & Company
Toronto

Unlikely Travels

Adventurers, us?

Not really, although we are extremely curious about other places, have an insatiable hunger for departures, and a pronounced taste for unusual destinations, relatively speaking. Over a period of twenty years we've worked together, for newspapers or books, putting our shared approach to travel to the test. What counts most is a good departure, no matter the destination. Travelling for the sake of travelling, in shared solitude made up of long silences and unexpected meetings. Each one in his own bubble, yet together, whether at the centre of the Mongolian steppe, the Arizona desert, or the Azerbaijan oil fields. *L'une*

chante, l'autre pas (*One Sings, the Other Doesn't*) is the title of an Agnès Varda film; in our case, we could say "One writes, the other draws." With time, we came to know one another well enough to anticipate the other's reactions, and considered recording them in duly thought-out books. We prize machines, whether they fly, drive or float. We've travelled on all of them and we continue in our aim of sharing our emotions with readers.

One cold night in Paris: others had an understandable desire to find the sun. Not us, having already assessed our innocent weakness for what is incorrectly called "bad weather." Georges Brassens sings about "idiotic countries where it never rains." An exposition on streamlining seen several months earlier in Montreal had reminded us that in Canada, there still existed a stainless steel train designed to cross the country. It bears the simple name of the *Canadian*, it would be impossible to be more explicit. According to the Internet, the train is easily accessible, and it's even expecting us.

As far as railways are concerned, the Trans-Siberian belongs to everyone, since Blaise Cendrars wrote his poem. Other trains with endless tracks cross the Australian continent, bits of Asia, entire swathes of southern Africa. In North America, it's logical that Canada, the largest of the nations, has at its disposal the most extensive stretch of tracks, more than four thousand kilometres between Toronto and Vancouver, falling across four time zones. The *Canadian* moves rather slowly and stops for several hours in the middle of the night, the exact opposite of the high-speed trains we're accustomed to in Europe. It's not a train taken by school children, but it is taken by workers as well as tourists. Its unhurried rhythm prompts dreaming, reminiscing, a certain melancholy always associated with temporary distance. Because, even without ever having travelled on this train, we are all familiar with the strange feeling that assails us when our gaze is carried out the window onto rising and falling electrical lines...

The *Canadian* offers us a passage, the passage sought after by the pioneers on the bumpy road to the mythical West, the sun, riches, freedom: from Toronto, the megalopolis open to all, to the infinite expanses of the Prairies, sown with wheat or ice, from the snowy peaks of the Rockies to Vancouver Bay, just as stunning as Naples or Rio. A journey suited to reading, writing, drawing (which we achieved with this book already in mind, perhaps the first in a series we've been considering for too long already). Unexpected journeys because they defy exoticism, even if they take place far, far away. The double gaze we offer here, the gaze of each of our pens, will take in every bit of the world, in lands where paths still remain to be cleared. Still, distance means nothing, space is linked to a pure construction of convenience. Time is what assails us. The passing of the hours is a much greater test than the passing of time zones. And, since everything does pass, let us make an effort to preserve a bit of it.

The trains are always shown backwards. The last car appears to be the first! (For a long time, I thought American and Canadian trains travelled in the opposite direction of French trains –

Les trains sont toujours présentés à l'envers. Le wagon de queue semble être le wagon de tête! (Pendant longtemps j'ai cru que les trains US et Canadiens roulaient en sens inverse des trains français –

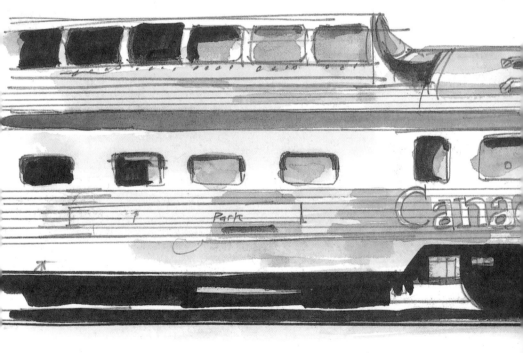

Park

Cana

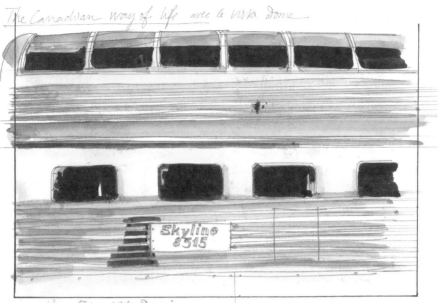

The Canadian way of life avec le Vista Dome

Skyline
#515

voitures "Type Vista Dome"
Je pense qu'elles ont été rachetées aux Américains vers 1961.

The Canadian way of life with the Vista Dome. "Vista Dome" type cars I think they were purchased from the Americans around 1961.

les subdivisions (Railway division pour
sont basées sur la distance que peut
parcourir une loco à vapeur en 1 jour)
les miles vont à 0 de l'Est vers l'Ouest

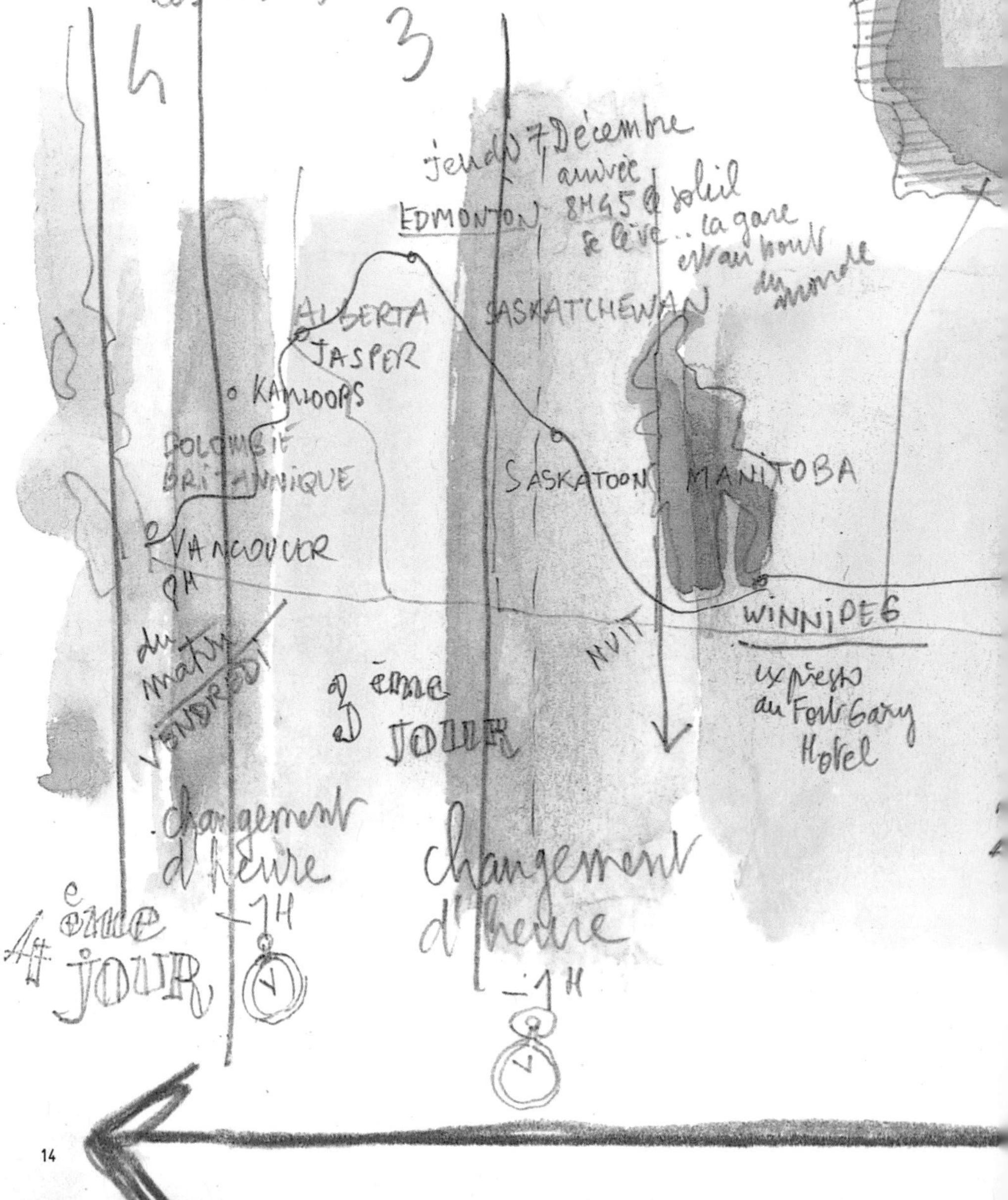

3

jeudi 7 Décembre
EDMONTON arrivée 8H45 @ soleil
se lève... la gare
est au bout
du monde

ALBERTA   SASKATCHEWAN
JASPER
o KAMLOOPS
COLOMBIE
BRITANNIQUE   SASKATOON   MANITOBA

o VANCOUVER
9H

du matin
VENDREDI   3ème
                JOUR   NUIT   WINNIPEG

                                         expresso
                                         au Fort Gary
changement   Hotel
d'heure
-1H   changement
           d'heure
4ème   -1H
JOUR,

The subdivisions (Railway division points, based on the distance a steam engine could cover in one day) The miles go from 0 in the East towards the West

1
1er JOUR
QUEBEC
ONTARIO
(775 miles)
SIOUX LOOKOUT
mercredi
6 Décembre
9H
rest. chinois
262 miles 16H35
CAPREOL
SUDBURY 276 mi
Dep 17H00.
TORONTO
Depart
mardi 5 Décembre
9H
JOUR
Changement d'heure
-1H
on déjeune
à 11H
on dîne
à 17H
au lit à 20H!

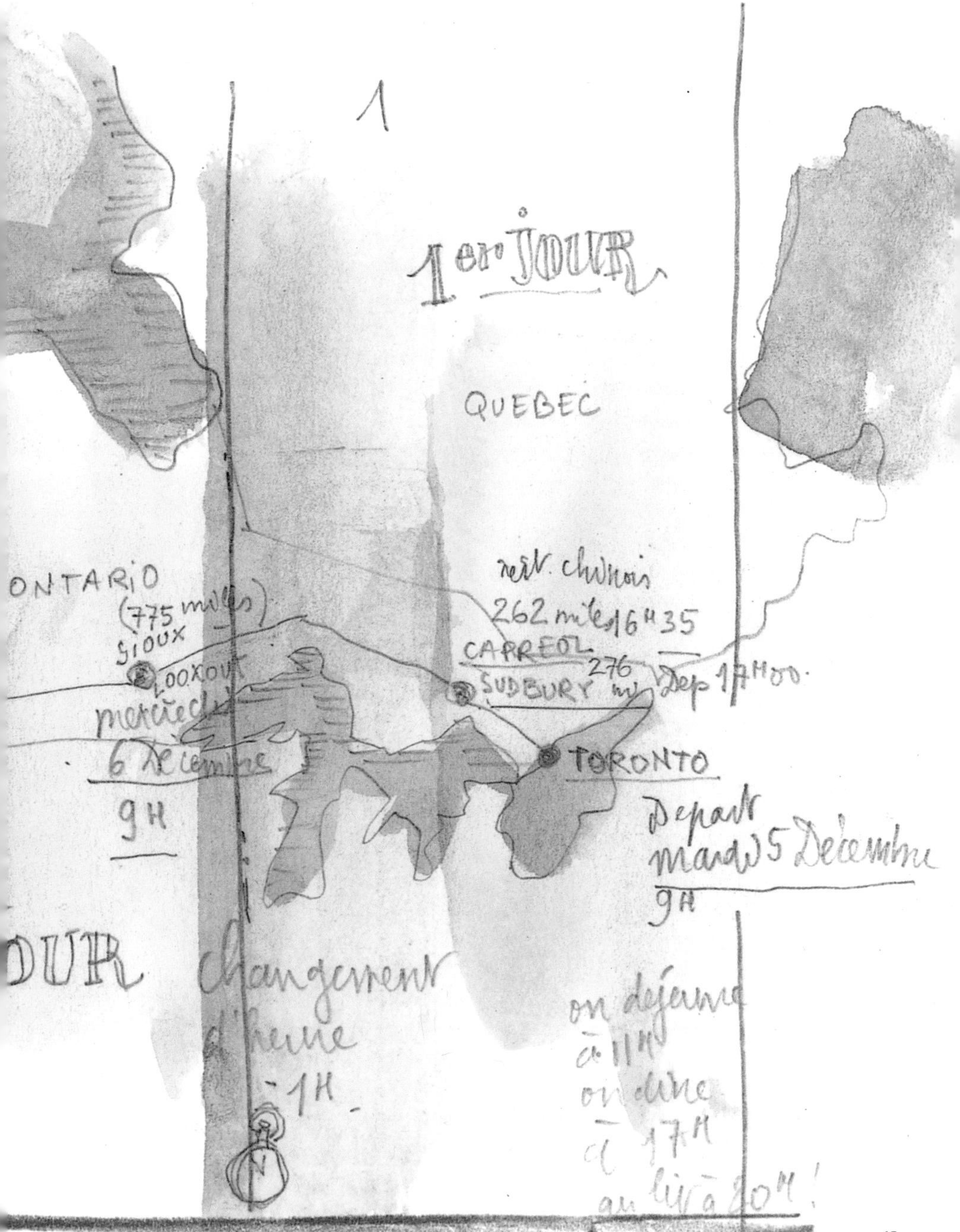

We'd heard about a train that travelled all the way across Canada.

"O Canada"

One could say: here is an expanse without visible limits, a majestic expanse, whose national anthem celebrates just this infiniteness. Voltaire's oft-repeated line reduces Canada to "a few snowy acres." The expression is too common, abusively simplistic. However, it does remind us of the bicentenary vision of a continental country that straddles the two major Occidental oceans, the Atlantic and the Pacific. A sovereign state nonetheless, that also has a sovereign, the Queen of England. A bilingual country, nominally at least, once divided into (Anglophone) Upper Canada and (Francophone) Lower Canada. French presence preceded its British rival's, even if the latter eventually won out. Lower Canada, a bit like France's *Seine-Inférieure* or the *Basse-Alps* which also wished to change their names to *Seine-Maritime* and *Alpes-de-Haute-Provence*. A rich, developed, in other words, modern, area that witnessed the confrontation of Old Europe's two major imperialist powers: France and Great Britain, and which, like Oceania's minuscule Vanuatu, the former "Franco-British Condominium," still officially retains language of each. Even though French well and truly prevailed in the East, to the point that it remains dominant by a large majority in Quebec and at near equality in New Brunswick, part of what was once *l'Acadie*, English reigns in the rest of the country. But who, in Europe, is aware of the francophone minorities living in every single one of the provinces, from Manitoba to British Columbia? A former French colony that became a member of the Commonwealth, Canada is expert in the art of conciliation: if choosing means abandoning something, it is undoubtedly better to adopt compatibility. Do Francophone Montreal and Anglophone Toronto see each other as rivals? The capital, then, will be established in Ottawa, halfway between the two cities, offering an example to be followed by Australia with Canberra, the arbitrator of the Sydney-Melbourne confrontation. A faithful ally of Great Britain, Canada paid dearly during the two world wars, but unites with the US, its strong southern neighbour in all kinds of fields: especially telecommunications and sports competitions. After all, a team from Toronto participates in the prestigious American NBA; at one time, Montreal tried its hand in the baseball league; and who doesn't know, by reputation at least, the glorious tricolour of the Montreal Canadiens, frequent winners of the Stanley Cup, ice hockey's supreme trophy. Ten provinces, three independent territories, ten million square kilometres, thirty-three million inhabitants: it's so much, and it's so little.

We knew most of all this after crossing the country by car several times and flying over it in planes as well. We had also heard about a train that travelled all the way across Canada, following the path taken by pioneers' wagons, with railroad tracks laid down in a land of prairies and lakes, and mountains, too – sort of American Trans-Siberian. We started to gather information on it and what we collected opened the door to the dream: the train still existed, it runs all year linking Toronto (Ontario) and Vancouver (British Columbia) in both directions, and it's relatively inexpensive. We could leave in any season, and we chose winter – Gilles Vigneault so aptly sang: "My country is not a country, it's winter!" Canada itself is not only brilliantly cold, but its ice and snow confer upon it its primary light and grandeur, which is perhaps even greater during the dazzling *été indien*, Indian Summer. Canadians prefer the expression *été des Indiens*, the Indians' Summer, which has advantages of its own. Autumn's brief symphony seems much more like a beginning than an end. But white won out over the roses of Lancaster and York. December in Toronto.

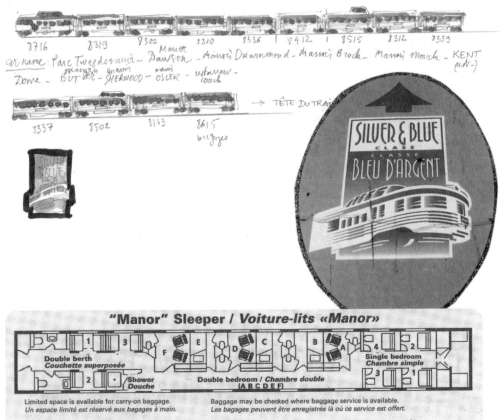

"Manor" Sleeper / Voiture-lits «Manor»

Double berth
Couchette superposée

Shower
Douche

Double bedroom / Chambre double
(A B C D E F)

Single bedroom
Chambre simple

Limited space is available for carry-on baggage.
Un espace limité est réservé aux bagages à main.

Baggage may be checked where baggage service is available.
Les bagages peuvent être enregistrés là où ce service est offert.

Bedrooms A+B, C+D and E+F can be combined into a suite. / Les chambres A et B, C et D, E et F peuvent être converties en suite.

We could leave in any season, and we chose winter.

VIA Rail Canada

APRIL 23, 1999   LE 23 AVRIL 1999

THE QUICK ACTIONS OF VIA RAIL ENGINEERS DON BLAIN, 45, AND KEVIN LIHOU, 33, JUST MOMENTS BEFORE THE DERAILMENT OF THEIR TRAIN, VIA 74, WERE INSTRUMENTAL IN AVOIDING THE POTENTIAL DEATH AND/OR INJURY TO NEARLY 300 PEOPLE IN TWO PASSENGER TRAINS. ENGINEERS BLAIN AND LIHOU ACTED HEROICALLY WHILE DISREGARDING THEIR PERSONAL SAFETY. IN SECONDS, THEY RECOGNIZED AN IMPROPERLY SET SWITCH, APPLIED THE BRAKES ON THEIR TRAIN, SHUT OFF THE ENGINE THEREBY REMOVING AN IGNITION SOURCE AND RADIOED A WARNING TO ANOTHER APPROACHING VIA TRAIN. DON BLAIN AND KEVIN LIHOU DIED IN THE DERAILMENT AND COLLISION ON APRIL 23, 1999. THEIR COURAGEOUS ACTIONS ON THAT DATE ARE RECOGNIZED AND COMMEMORATED BY THIS PLAQUE.

LA RÉACTION RAPIDE DE MM. DON BLAIN, 45 ANS, ET KEVIN LIHOU, 33 ANS, MÉCANICIENS DE LOCOMOTIVE DE VIA RAIL, QUELQUES SECONDES AVANT LE DÉRAILLEMENT DE LEUR TRAIN VIA 74, A SAUVÉ LA VIE ET ÉVITÉ LES BLESSURES À PRÈS DE 300 PERSONNES SE TROUVANT À BORD DE DEUX TRAINS DE VOYAGEURS. MM. BLAIN ET LIHOU ONT AGI AVEC HÉROÏSME EN FAISANT FI DE LEUR SÉCURITÉ PERSONNELLE. EN À PEINE QUELQUES SECONDES, ILS ONT REPÉRÉ UN ARGUIFFAGE MAL RÉGLÉ, SERRÉ LE FREIN D'URGENCE, ARRÊTÉ LE MOTEUR, ÉVITANT PAR LÀ UN INCENDIE, ET AVERTI L'ÉQUIPE D'UN TRAIN VIA VENANT EN SENS INVERSE. DON BLAIN ET KEVIN LIHOU SONT DÉCÉDÉS DANS CE DÉRAILLEMENT ET LA COLLISION SURVENUS LE 23 AVRIL 1999. LEUR COURAGE CE JOUR-LÀ EST RECONNU ET COMMÉMORÉ PAR LA PRÉSENTE PLAQUE.

PAUL M. TELLIER   ROD MORRISON
PRESIDENT AND CEO/PDG   PRESIDENT/PRÉSIDENT
CN   VIA RAIL

Tuesday, December 5th
Departure from Toronto: 9:00

mardi 5 Décembre

Départ TORONTO : 9.00

In order to do things just right, we stayed at the Royal York hotel, built between 1928 and 1929 by the Canadian Pacific Railway company.

It's snowing. This is what we were hoping for.

Toronto

It's snowing. This is what we were hoping for. The flurries turn Lester B. Pearson Airport white, only the runways have been cleared. Lake Ontario shivers, ice has not yet besieged it. Next to us, the mango-coloured DHL plane pushes back. We hardly feel the sting of the wind, a taxi carries us downtown. State of extreme enthusiasm. Tomorrow we begin our westward journey of three days and three nights, crossing half the Canadian provinces, passing through three time zones to cover 4,500 kilometres. Abstractions about to become realities. In order to do things just right, we stayed at the Royal York Hotel, built between 1928 and 1929 by the Canadian Pacific Railway Company, which already owned the property across the street, Union Station, erected ten years previous in the same massive style and with pinkish rubble-stones, crowned with the inscription "Anno Domini MCMXIX." For many years, the most significant hotel of the Commonwealth, The Royal York belongs to the category of establishments that North Americans call "landmark hotels," in other words, places where history has unfolded. A very British atmosphere reigns in the lobbies and common areas, similar constructions exist in Melbourne or Wellington. A certain kind of cosy comfort, dark wood, subdued lighting, the soothing ritual of cocktails...

Is it because the Christmas holidays are so close? The Royal York's shopping area, in the basement, has an abundance of toy stores offering a most attractive array of miniatures from around the world: automobiles, ships, planes, trains. The shops close one by one, businessmen hurry, thinking of their children, the restaurants empty out. We go out to have an Indian dinner at the foot of the CN Tower. In the dark, the storm seems to worsen as we walk back. From my room, on the eighteenth floor, I can barely make out the lake beyond the road that runs alongside it, the elevated highway, headlights pierce holes in the curtain of snow falling noiselessly. I must confess that such quilted landscapes, softened tones, with an atmosphere belonging to both day and night, between wakefulness and sleep, always have a peaceful effect on me.

We crammed to learn our material. The idea of a railway linking the East and West of the country goes back to the 1870s. The Canadian Confederation, created in 1867, is still divided at that time, some provinces (British Columbia) are considering seceding, others (Manitoba) only exist in theory, and the population is concentrated around the Great Lakes and the Saint-Lawrence River. The first Conservative Prime Minister, John Alexander Macdonald and Quebec's George-Etienne Cartier anticipate that a railway line would contribute not only to the feeling of being a nation, but also to the necessary settling of immigrants and business. In a few years' time (1881-1886), the Canadian Pacific Railway (PC), run by W.C. Van Horne, performs the gargantuan undertaking, despite the devastating avalanches. Monumental hotels, resembling the châteaux along the Loire River or fortified Tudor manors, flourish in the stopover cities – Winnipeg, Calgary, Banff. The Rockies are transformed into mountain vacation resorts, adventurers like Jack London mix with the very British gentry, who are enamoured of this train, a contemporary of the Orient Express, soon to be mirrored in part by the rival Canadian National Railway (CN) line that passes farther north, through Edmonton and Jasper. During the 1920s and 30s, the art deco décor and the sumptuous locomotives, the *Mountain VI*, the *Royal Hudson*, and later the

Selkirk Class delight travellers. Today, diesel has replaced steam. We must admit that, to us, this train looks quite a lot like a life-size toy. We've always loved them, motorized miniature cars, planes or railways. Still, the utilitarian look of the *Canadian* is not what charms us on board. Rather, we'll be living cut off from the world, as if we were the heroes of this life-sized dream.

A dossier prepared by Via Rail, the company that resulted from the 1978 merge of CP's passenger line and CN and which has since run the *Canadien/Canadian*, was brought to my hotel room. Most importantly, it contains my Toronto–Vancouver ticket in Silver and Blue Class. Departing from Toronto, Tuesday at 9 o'clock, arriving in Vancouver, Friday at 7:50. A 'single' compartment awaits me (in Canada, they write *chambre simple*). A menu, a schedule, a variety of instructions fill the folder. We will be stopping in stations whose names are unknown to me: Gogama, Sioux Lookout, Winnitoba, Portage la Prairie. Half the kilometres of the Trans-Siberian: not bad. We are about to step into a poem of proper names where Native American

sounds mingle with the sounds of English and French. A kind of onomastic symphony.

Front Street separates the Royal York from Union Station. The early morning is freezing, but the station is heated, like all buildings in Canada. A bit like New York's Grand Central on a smaller scale. An engraved frieze runs along under the glass roof, listing the cities served. The departure board: train No. 1 is our train. After a warm welcome in a private lounge, we are escorted to the platform, to car 8322, dubbed "Drummond Manor." It's low season, there are only thirteen cars, as opposed to thirty-three in the summer. There are few passengers, on board great care is taken stowing the baggage, and to accompany the formalities, we are introduced to the travelling personnel: a ritual inspired by first-class airplane travel, which the train claimed to rival until competition became too great. Even more surprising to us is the procedure called "the turn-around triangle" which is explained to us in detail as dating back to the electoral campaigns of the 1930s. The candidate's train would pass the station where the welcome committee was waiting for him and slowly come back in reverse: the last car then arrives first, and it is equipped with an open platform from which the hero of the day greets the crowd. In memory of this, the personnel continues, North American trains are usually depicted from the rear, unlike Old World trains where the locomotive normally occupies the privileged foreground.

Here we are in our "room," along both sides of the central aisle. Austere and minimalist. The sink-washroom takes up space, but the picture window literally serves the view up to us. Let's get comfortable, though we're measuring our movements, let's get to know this cabin, our universe for the seventy-one hours to come.

Here we are, each in his own space, before we leave, we're reading the mountain of documentation we have at our disposal on Canada, its railways, their history, their style, beginning with streamlining or aerodynamics, that North America industrial aesthetic of the 1930s and 40s, born of the precepts of Bauhaus applied to home economics and to transportation as well. Movement, ergonomics, fluidity; streamlining leads to a style of living based on speed, beauty, the exaltation of modern times. As America emerges bruised from the crises of the 1930s, the Chrysler Building, the Empire State Building and others like them outline a renàissance in New York, the city that was most hurt, and that is the most symbolic. Raymond Loewy theorizes on the shape of locomotives and affirms that ugliness doesn't sell well. Our *Canadian* offers the perfect application of this: the rounded shape of both the cars and the furniture, the pre-eminence of moulded stainless steel, and windowed surfaces, a raised, panoramic observation deck at both the front and rear of the train: the VistaDome. Truly, the whole thing has an attractive look in the sun and cold of this winter morning, and this concentration of semi-secular high technology offers the same pleasure as driving a Cadillac or a Packard from the height of that era.

We're leaving Toronto, this other New York, which, as cosmopolitan as its older counterpart, has become Canada's economic capital. The French are all too unfamiliar with this place, just as they are with Chicago. Yet each of these cities makes the most of the advantages of its lakeside situation and its never-disappointing taste for avant-garde architecture. The *Canadian*'s now on its way, and, beyond the glass of Union Station which had hidden the skyline, Toronto's towering buildings appear, along with its water towers, those blackened wood tanks that are so familiar in New York. The bell rings at a suburban level crossing, we pass into the natural landscape that will be our principal setting for the length of the trip, plains, lakes, forests.

CN TOWER LA TOUR CN
CANADA'S WONDER OF THE WORLD   NOTRE MERVEILLE DU MONDE

OBS+SKY POD
OBS+NACELLE

Look Out/Belvédère

Glass Floor/
    Plancher de verre

Sky Pod/Nacelle

ADMIT ONE/UNE ADMISSION

A/A

VALID/VALABLE: 06/12/04

Ticket is valid for one visit only
Billet valable pour une seule visite

No Resale Value/Aucune valeur de revente

VOTRE ID DU PHOTO
CN TOWER
CANADA'S WONDER OF THE WORLD
LA TOUR CN
NOTRE MERVEILLE DU MONDE

Merci
pour donner nous l'occasion de vous photographier.
Vous pourriez voir et acheter votre photo à notre galerie
contigue au Marketplace Café à la base de la Tour.

Date _____   Photo ID #_____ 1340

SharpShooter Imaging, Inc.
11901 West 48th Avenue, Suite 200
Wheat Ridge, CO 80033 • 800-637-3686

SharpShooter
Imaging

We're leaving Toronto, this other New York, which, as cosmopolitan as its older counterpart, has become Canada's economic capital.

447 m The Sky Pod, the world's highest observation deck

447 m le s k y pod
la galerie d'observation
la plus élevée du monde.

553,33 mètres

Beyond the glass of Union Station which had hidden
the skyline, Toronto's towering buildings appear.(Left)

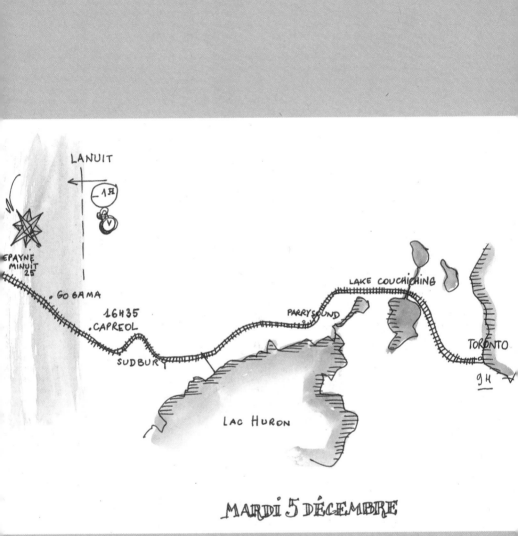

MARDI 5 DÉCEMBRE

Tuesday December 5th

9 heures... on est partis

9 o'clock ... we're on our way.

Skyline Car

Scenic Dome

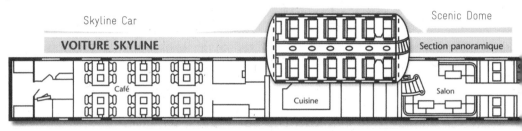

VOITURE SKYLINE

Section panoramique

Café

Cuisine

Salon

VOITURE PARC

Les chambres C+D peuvent être converties en suite.

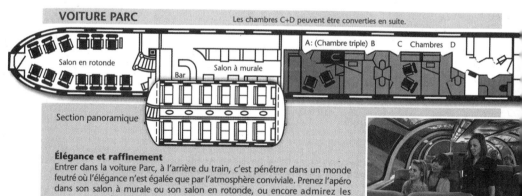

Salon en rotonde

Bar

Salon à murale

A: (Chambre triple) B   C   Chambres   D

Section panoramique

Élégance et raffinement

Entrer dans la voiture Parc, à l'arrière du train, c'est pénétrer dans un monde feutré où l'élégance n'est égalée que par l'atmosphère conviviale. Prenez l'apéro dans son salon à murale ou son salon en rotonde, ou encore admirez les paysages environnants depuis sa section panoramique à l'étage.

Panoramas and Elegance

The Park Car, at the rear of the train, is a whole new world, a peaceful environment combining elegance and comfort. Enjoy a cocktail in the Mural Lounge or the Bullet Lounge, or even admire the surrounding vistas from the upper-level Scenic Dome.

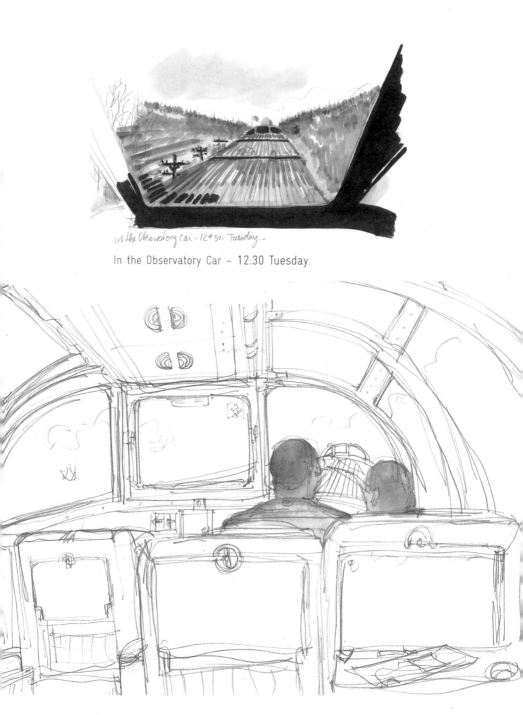

In the Observatory Car – 12:30 Tuesday.

voiture de queue
jeudi

Last car Thursday

"RCMP
Boss
Quits"
Edmonton
Journal
↓

8716

Little by little, 1940s and 50s luxury trains adopt enclosed observation cars. Always situated at the rear of the train, these carriages are something of a figurehead, they are often quite stylized and, in an effort to underscore their modernism, certain companies decorate them with rocket-style flaps or space capsule portholes.

Les trains de luxe des années 1940 et 1950 adoptent peu à peu des « observation cars » fermées. Toujours placées en queue de train, ces voitures constituent en quelque sorte une figure de poupe, souvent très stylisée, certaines compagnies, pour marquer leur modernisme, allant jusqu'à les décorer avec des ailerons de fusée ou des hublots de capsule spatiale.

voiture de queue
la montée d'escalier
a l'observatory 200m

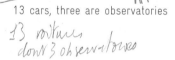

13 cars, three are observatories

13 voitures
dont 3 observatoires

Streamlining or aerodynamics, that North America industrial aesthetic of the 1930s and 40s, born of the precepts of Bauhaus.

le salon rotonde — The Bullet Lounge

Keepsakes

Excerpt from the western souvenir catalogue
Whistle: $10 ($11.50 on the train)
Whistle: the sound recalls the whistle of an
old steam locomotive.

Lapel pin $3.50

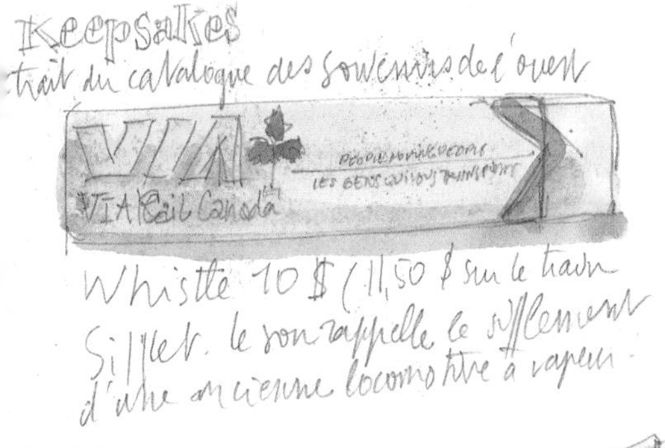

Keepsakes
trait du catalogue des souvenirs de l'ouest

Whistle 10 $ (11,50 $ sur le train
Sifflet. le son rappelle le sifflement
d'une ancienne locomotive à vapeur.

épingle
de revers
3.50 $

Stylo le bouchon du stylo
comporte la même
image que les aimants 2 $
No 850939 stylo - paysage de montagne
avec le Canadien

Pen:
the pen cap has
the same picture
as the magnets $2
No. 850939 pen –
mountain view
from the *Canadian*

14,00 $

cuillère
de
collection
6,85 $

casquette
de
mecanicien
de
locomotive

Collectible spoon $6.85

Engineer's Cap $14.00

381 meters
These are The Mond Nickel Company's two smokestacks
Sudbury (+262 miles from the starting point)

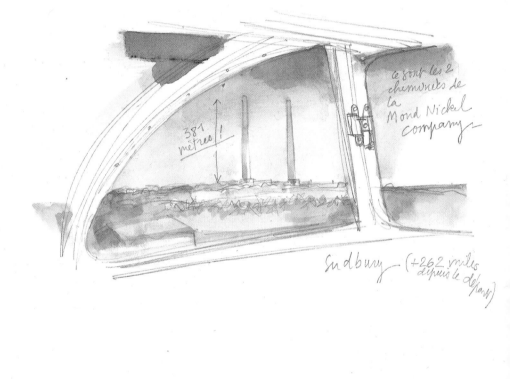

VIA Rail Canada

DRUMMOND MANOR   8322   *MANOIR DRUMMOND*

William Henry Drummond, FRSC. (1854-1907) whose name this car bears, gained fame as a poet in French-Canadian dialect. A practicing physician in Montreal, he published several volumes of widely quoted verse, notably "The Habitant", "Johnnie Courteau" and "The Voyageur".

William Henry Drummond, membre de l'Académie des Sciences du Canada (1854-1907), dont cette voiture porte le nom, est devenu célèbre pour ses poèmes en français canadien. Médecin pratiquant à Montréal, il a publié plusieurs volumes de poésie fréquemment cités, notamment The Habitant, Johnnie Courteau et The Voyageur.

Come fly with me
Harry Connick Jr.
&
The Sea (Charles T.!)
and
Michael Bublé
(Heaven by Paul Anka?)
Home

Souvenir Car with Gary

Compliments of Via

Three o'clock tea

63

Wednesday December 6

mercredi 6 Décembre

Sioux Lookout
Winnipeg
Portage la Prairie

Sioux Lookout

Winnipeg

Portage
la Prairie

MANITOBA

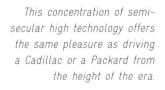

This concentration of semi-secular high technology offers the same pleasure as driving a Cadillac or a Packard from the height of the era.

Quite rare in a train ...
a shower!

Not bad at all: the
stall is spacious and
the water nice and hot

assez rare
dans un train :
une douche !

(Finalement plutôt bien :
la cabine est spacieuse et l'eau bien chaude !)

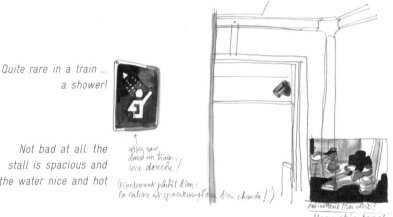

Robinetterie très chic !
Very chic taps!

December 6th **6 Décembre**
Daybreak

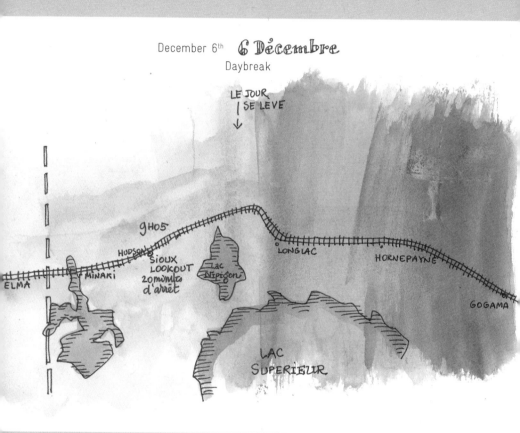

LE JOUR
SE LEVE
↓

9H05

HUDSON

SIOUX
LOOKOUT
20 minutes
d'arrêt

ELMA

MINAKI

Lac
Nipigon

LONGLAC

HORNEPAYNE

GOGAMA

LAC
SUPÉRIEUR

69

Eastern Time
Heure de l'ESA

Central Time
Heure du Centre

Mountain Time
Heure des Rocheuses

This is the hill where the Ojibway watched the Sioux

c'est de cette colline que les Ojibway surveillaient les sioux –

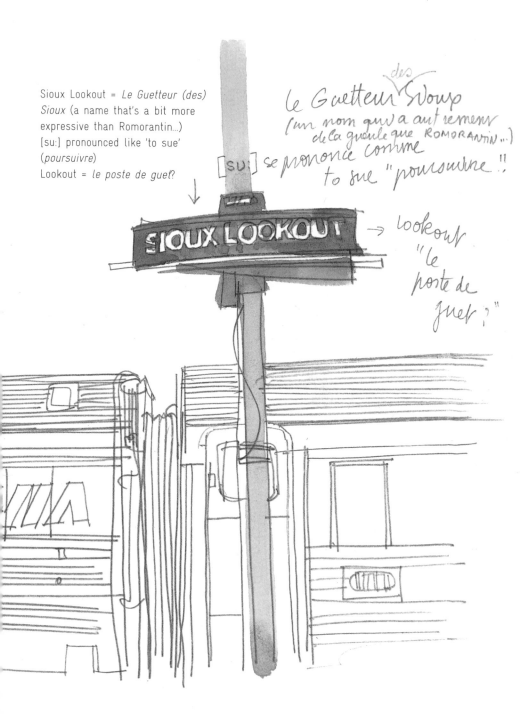

Sioux Lookout = *Le Guetteur (des) Sioux* (a name that's a bit more expressive than Romorantin...)
[su:] pronounced like 'to sue' (*poursuivre*)
Lookout = *le poste de guet*?

SIOUX LOOKOUT

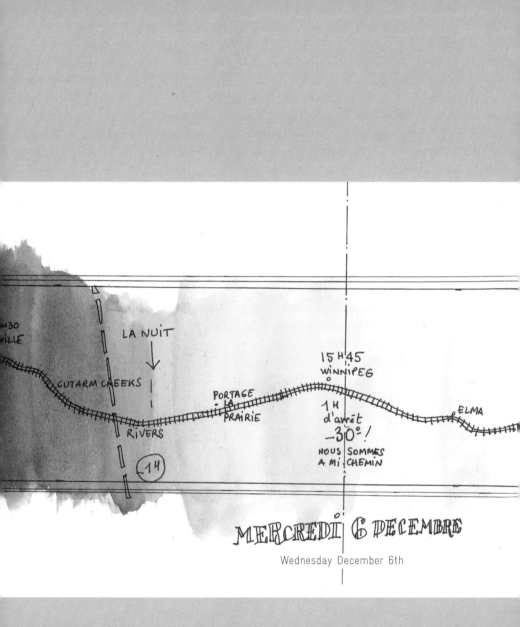

H30
VILLE

LA NUIT
↓

CUTARM CREEKS

RIVERS

-1H

15H45
WINNIPEG
°

PORTAGE
- LA
PRAIRIE

1H
d'arrêt
-30°!
NOUS SOMMES
A MI-CHEMIN

ELMA

MERCREDI 6 DECEMBRE

Wednesday December 6th

Ontario

The province of Ontario, twice as big as France with six times fewer people, crossed from east to west represents just a bit less than half the trip. At the edge of Lake Simcoe, a farm flanked by its navy blue silo at the foot of which is parked a bright red pick-up truck. Parry Sound is built on Georgian Bay, at the extreme north-east point of Lake Huron, one of the five Great Lakes. Thirty thousand islands in the Bay. We notice other stretches of water with Native names pronounced by the conductor: Nipissing, Kakagiwizida, Wanapitei. Perhaps these consonants and vowels designate magical places, the melody born from uttering them could make us believe we're in the heart of Africa. The smoke from Sudbury darkens the clear sky: blast furnaces, copper and nickel, working class suburbs. It's time to take our places at the dining table, eating is the one activity all the others hinge on, it is meticulously seen to by the staff and prized by all the travellers. Everything is indeed conceived to break the inevitable monotony, accentuated by the low speed – an average of sixty kilometres an hour – and the brevity of winter days. Thus the maître d' never seats us at the same table and suggests that for each meal we alternate between the two possible times, in order to have different neighbours: British retirees, a Mexican backpacker, Ontario residents. The *Canadian* isn't anything like a private luxury train, it belongs to a public company and serves its clients. This is how we met a politician who has an airplane phobia, on his way home from the Liberal Party Convention. The meal selections are varied, tasty, abundant, without pretension, and they offer a pretext for alcohol-accompanied extensions, especially at dinner: night falls at about five o'clock.

Here we are in Capreol, a small town constructed by the builders of the line, where some of their descendants settled. A main street, a few closed shops, lighted signs. It looks like Painful Gulch, or any one of the lost towns of the West that comic-book hero Lucky Luke finds himself in. We wouldn't be surprised to see Rantanplan and the Dalton Brothers, a sheriff or a barber appear. In our childhoods, Morris' hero offered us an approximate and attractive idea of America, as did Hergé's comic book about Chicago gangsters. A half hour stop. The only business that's open, Lucky Luke still, a Chinese restaurant and take-out establishment accustomed to the *Canadian's* three stops per week, supplying the Peking Palace – telephone 858-1007 – with passengers who are hungry or just tired of the onboard cuisine. As usual, an entire family runs the place, it's perfectly organized. In the dark, we make our way back to our mobile rooms, bellies filled with Cantonese rice and chicken chop suey.

The Nemegosenda River, the Obakamiga River, the Kenogami River, Saint Joseph's Church, completely yellow, in Ferland, the Chapleau and Wakami Parks, McDougall Bay's windmill in ruins, the Sturgeon Viaduct, Sioux Lookout's Tudor-style train station, each filed by in the Native American landscape. Is this Native language written? We don't know. Someone tells us that at the entrance to First Nations Park, there's a welcome sign written in English and in Oji-Cree, the local language. In my mind appear images of a Native reserve outside Montreal, with its idle population supported by Social Assistance, witness of a time that is gone forever, linked to the past and whose prospects of a future are impossible to imagine.

ma voisine
en
1959

← *My neighbour in 1959.*

ma voisine
en
2006
→

My neighbour in 2006.

Amérique Winnipeg. On dirait un Hopper.

Arrival in Winnipeg. It looks like a Hopper painting.

WINNIPEG

Manitoba, Saskatchewan

The "Manitoba" is not answering, the title of a comic book by Hergé: Jo, Zette and Jocko are investigating the disappearance of a steamliner that left New York on its way to Liverpool. For a long time, this was perhaps the only reason we had to cite the Algonquin name of this central province of the Canadian Prairies, whose northern edge borders Hudson Bay. In the middle of the second day, we left Ontario and entered Manitoba, which doesn't look much different. After a short while, in the distance, on the plain, appear the buildings of Winnipeg, the capital of the province, at the confluence of the Red and the Assiniboine rivers. These names stir the imagination with some movie memories. Isn't Red River one of the world's most lyrical westerns, and in River of No Return, don't Marilyn's perfect legs crossing the current transport us?

But the suburbs are not to be outdone: we cross the Seine, yes indeed, as it flows through Saint-Boniface, a francophone city opposite Winnipeg. No one, or nearly no one, in Europe is aware of the existence of the Franco-Manitobans, a micro-community that is alive and well and gave birth to at least one recognized author: Gabrielle Roy. Winner of the Prix Femina in 1947 for Bonheur d'occasion, she lived near the cathedral, on the tiny rue Deschambault, also the title of a collection of short stories. Her house has become a museum, we had just enough time to take a quick look, the *Canadian* only stops in Winnipeg for an hour: a two-storey house, typical of French Canada, warm and refined.

We make our way quickly back to Union Station, but not without a brief stop in the Fort Garry Hotel, another landmark with a greenish bronze roof, where an Italian-style espresso is more than welcome. Cold reigns here: minus thirty-five degrees.

From the Observation Car, we contemplate the orangey sky. Suddenly it turns night blue under the full moon. The horizon has become broader, the nocturnal sky envelops us. We have a fleeting sensation that we are part of something bigger: metaphysical in Manitoba? Between the cars, snow-drifts have formed, during the night, we'll go from the province of Manitoba into the province of Saskatchewan, though we won't see much of it. The station in Saskatoon, its largest city, seems closed when we stop there during the night. I remember another trip in Saskatchewan, not so many years ago. After arriving in Regina, the capital, I'd driven for miles across the treeless, frozen prairie, swept by a powdery wind that transformed the landscape into a mirage. There were still, I was told, Francophone towns in Saskatchewan – Gravelbourg, Belle-garde, Ponteix – inhabited by people from Québec. When I'd finally arrived, exhausted, one Sunday, all the inhabitants were attending mass at Notre-Dame de Ponteix. I was expected, and the priest interrupted his sermon to greet my arrival, discreet as it was, in his church ...

Ici les chevaux regardent passer les trains...

Here, horses watch the trains go by.

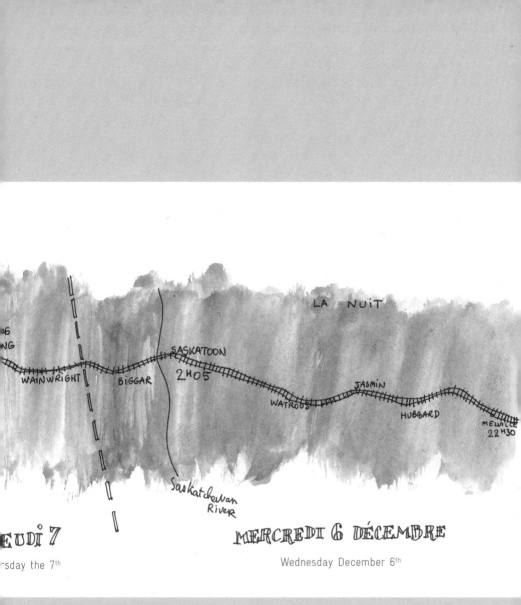

LA NUIT

SASKATOON
2H05

JASMIN
WATROUS
HUBBARD
MELVILLE
22H30

WAINWRIGHT   BIGGAR

Saskatchewan
River

EUDI 7

sday the 7th

MERCREDI 6 DÉCEMBRE

Wednesday December 6th

*From the Observation Car, we contemplate the orangey
sky. Suddenly it turns night blue under the full moon.*

Jeudi 7 Décembre

Edmonton   *Edmonton*
Jasper   *Jasper*
Velemount *Valemount*

Thursday December 7th

Jeudi 7 Décembre

Leaving Edmonton
The freight trains are
gigantic. Sometimes
pulled by four engines

Départ d'Edmonton
les trains de marchandises
sont gigantesques. Tirés
parfois par 4 locomotives

9 o'clock,
day breaks

9h
le jour
se lève

dans le Dôme de l'Observatory car

In the Dome of the Observatory Car

Built May 89
Series No. A-4849
BB Type
Diesel power V-16
cylinders
3000 horsepower

Fabriqué le
5-89.

Type BB -
Diesel 16 cylindres
en V- 3000ch

n° série - A-4849

GM Locomotive Group

6448

6448

les machines sont
des F40 PH. 2
la puissance de
traction est
obtenue par
2 machines
en tête du
train
(surtout pour
le franchissement
des
Rocheuses)

VIA

Canada

The engines are
F40Ph.2
The pulling force is
obtained by two loco-
motives at the front
of the train (needed
to cross the Rockies)

- NOS AGENTS A EDMONTON -
Us in Edmonton

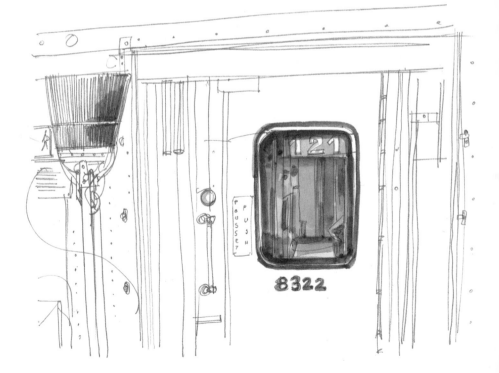

E. Edmonston

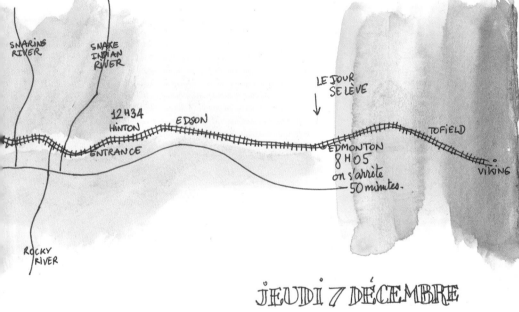

SNARING RIVER

SNAKE INDIAN RIVER

12434
HINTON   EDSON
ENTRANCE

ROCKY RIVER

LE JOUR SE LEVE

EDMONTON
8H05
on s'arrête
50 minutes.

TOFIELD

VIKING

JEUDI 7 DÉCEMBRE
Thursday December 7th

Before us, as we remain in the valley, the majestic mass
of the Rockies rises up.

The gem of the Rockies"

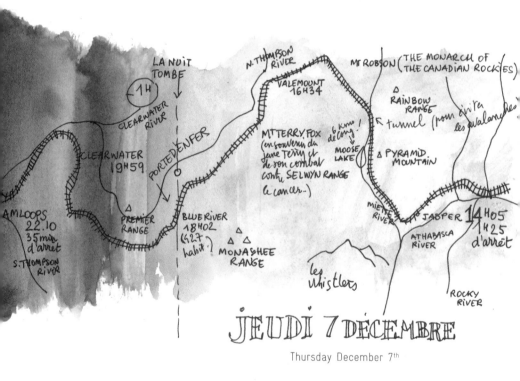

LA NUIT
TOMBE
1H

CLEARWATER RIVER

N.THOMPSON RIVER

VALEMOUNT
16H34

Mt ROBSON (THE MONARCH OF
THE CANADIAN ROCKIES)

△ RAINBOW
RANGE

← tunnel (pour éviter
les avalanches)

CLEARWATER
19H59

PORTE DE L'ENFER

Mt TERRY.FOX
(en souvenir du
jeune Terry et
de son combat
contre
le cancer...)

6 kms!
de long!

MOOSE
LAKE

SELWYN RANGE

△ PYRAMID
MOUNTAIN

KAMLOOPS
22.10
35min
d'arrêt

S.THOMPSON
RIVER

PREMIER
RANGE

BLUE RIVER
18H02
(627
habit.)

△ △
△
MONASHEE
RANGE

MIETTE
RIVER

JASPER

ATHABASCA
RIVER

14H05
H25
d'arrêt

les
Whistlers

ROCKY
RIVER

JEUDI 7 DÉCEMBRE

Thursday December 7th

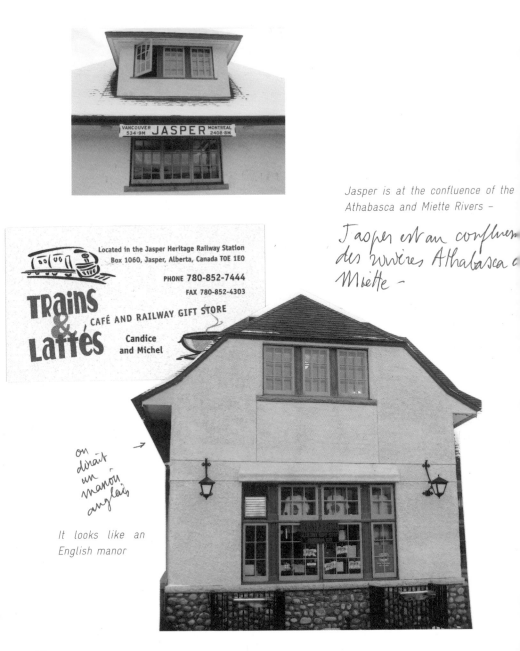

VANCOUVER 534·9M **JASPER** MONTREAL 2408·8M

Located in the Jasper Heritage Railway Station
Box 1060, Jasper, Alberta, Canada T0E 1E0

PHONE **780-852-7444**

FAX 780-852-4303

TRains & Laffés

CAFÉ AND RAILWAY GIFT STORE

Candice and Michel

Jasper is at the confluence of the
Athabasca and Miette Rivers –

*Jasper est au confluent
des rivières Athabasca e
Miette –*

*on dirait
un manou
anglais*

It looks like an
English manor

CANADIAN
NATIONAL
RAILWAYS

Travel
by train

SAF
COM

LIONEL

Railroad
2002
SHIRAZ CABERNET SAU
STERN CAPE

RAHAM BECK

GRAHAM BECK
SOUTH AFRICA

Leaving Jasper, we pass the totem pole of Whistler's (2470 m)

quittant Jasper on passe le long des Whistlers (2470 m)

Alberta, British Columbia

It was too dark for us to catch anything more than a glimpse of the Ukrainian church in Holden, with its silver, lighted dome. We've just crossed into the province of Alberta, the richest in Canada, because of the treasures, especially oil, found in the soil, that make it susceptible to separatist sirens. Defiant, like all the Western provinces, towards the cultural demands of the East, starting with French-speaking Québec. Edmonton, its capital, emerges in the distance; the station where the *Canadian* stops is at quite a distance, we won't have time to go take a look. Upon frozen lakes, the train's shadow is outlined, the forest becomes more dense, the hills rise imperceptibly, as

we go by Hinton, "the gateway to the Rockies," cross the Athabasca River on a suspension bridge and arrive in Jasper, a welcome stop of an hour and a half. The high peaks seem to be within arm's reach, pines reign supreme, these are the mountains, grandiose and taciturn.

Before us, as we remain in the valley, the majestic mass of the Rockies rises up. Jasper National Park, its sleigh rides and snowshoe hikes, all the winter sports are available to visitors. No time. Over them, we choose the wonderful shop occupying Jasper's western station, called the "Rail Café, Trains and Lattés". A dream for train lovers, real ones (all those books) and toys (all those miniatures) alike. But we didn't miss Mount Robson, the highest peak in the Canadian Rockies, reaching nearly four thousand meters, nor the Pyramid Waterfall or Hell's Gate Tunnel.

At around six the next morning, the air is damp and temperate. We are nearing the terminus, Vancouver, British Columbia. From a majestic suspended bridge, a myriad of red lights arise from the blue night: car traffic heading for the Western metropolis, whose population makes it as Asian as it is American, and which, unlike Greece's port city Pireas, bears the name of a man, in this case, one George Vancouver, an eighteenth century sailor. The journey ends at the Pacific Central Station, completed in 1919.

We disembark from the *Canadian*, the staff comes to say goodbye, we purchase the souvenir whistle. The building is deserted at this early hour, and we're feeling a bit strange, somewhat numb and disoriented. Return to the real world, the world of the sedentary, which we managed to escape from for a few days, but we're not travelling anymore, the game is over. Now we've come to a stop. Fleeting impression: Vancouver, Asian already, won't have to do very much to embrace and seduce us, cosmopolitan as it is. Opposite, in the Bay, Victoria Island. It is reached by a five minute flight, on small, ruddy yellow or red planes. We couldn't resist them.

The Rockies
Thursday 1:30 PM

les Rodimses
jeudi 13h30

depuis le 1½ on
ne peut plus
monter dans
la locomotive ...

Since 9/11 it's no longer possible to visit the engine

118

At night, watches are set back exactly one hour from Yellowhead Pass
(Alberta, British Colombia)

Ce soir on recule les montres d'une heure à l'aplomb de la Yellowhead Pass
(Alberta / British Columbia)

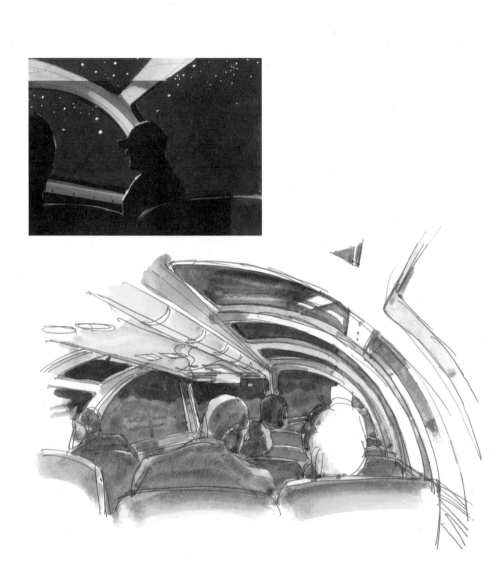

Friday December 8th

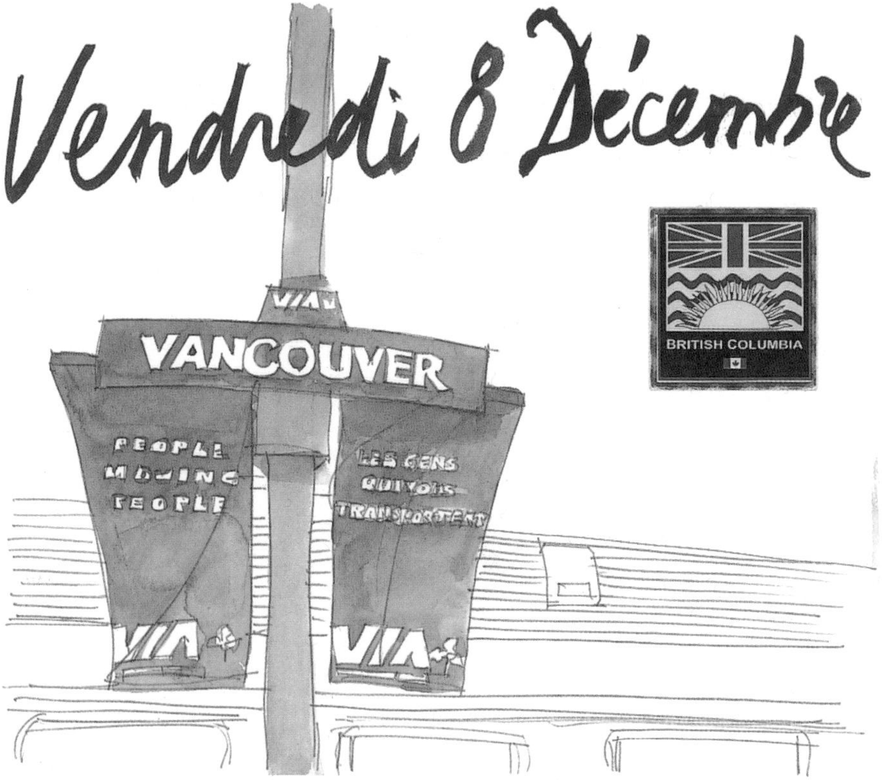

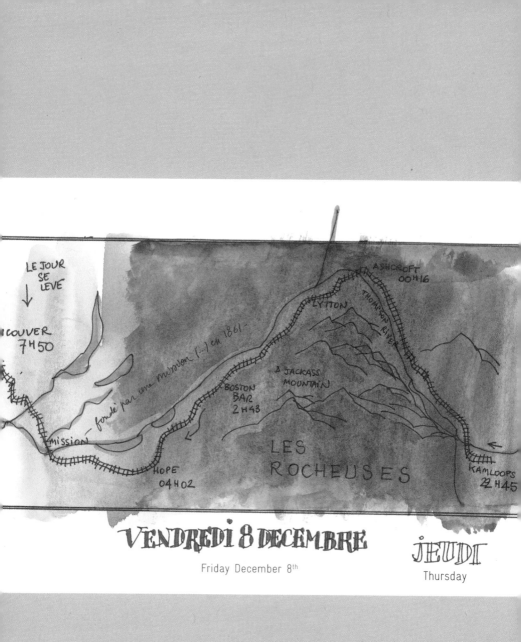

VENDREDI 8 DECEMBRE

Friday December 8th

JEUDI

Thursday

etiquette
verte:
Edmonton

Green tag:
Edmonton

VIA NO
VIA Rail Canada MD

082573

94

EDMONTON

Baggage Check / Bulletin de bagages

The baggage car (front of the train)

le wagon à bagages (en tête)

The journey was the destination

Vancouver

We disembark from the Canadian, and we're feeling
a bit strange, somewhat numb and disoriented.

**NCLOSURE
OTS À BAGGAGES**

Pour obtenir un remboursement
veuillez retournez votre chariot
au dépot le plus proche.

Plus de chariots sur L'Estrade
de Platform L'Autobus.   *Merci*

Le bilinguisme n'est pas toujours évident...
Bilingualism isn't always easy.

Above Saskatchewan

au dessus de
Saskatchewan

EMBARQUEMENT
A TORONTO
(en huron : "endroit où l'on se réunit)

Boarding for Toronto (in Huron: "the place where people come together")

Class | Classe
ECONOMY CLASS / CLASSE ECONOMIQUE

AIR CANADA

Flight & Date | Vol et date

AC 880 09DEC

Gate | Porte

ET

Seat | Place

28K

Where not prohibited by law
Sauf où la loi l'interdit

Boarding time
Heure d'embarquement

CNX ▶ 17:40

From | De

TORONTO-T1   EQ

To | Destination

PARIS-CDG-2

Name | Nom

BOULDOUYRE

Airline use | À usage interne

0057A   YVR64843

Boarding Pass | Carte d'accès à bord

↖ ma parka

my parka

Practical Information

TORONTO-JASPER-VANCOUVER TRAIN (*THE CANADIAN*)

The Canadian links **Toronto** and **Vancouver**, crossing the lake regions of northern Ontario, **the Western Prairies**, and the **Rocky Mountains**, concluding its path on the **Pacific Coast**. Stops are scheduled in Sudbury, Winnipeg, Saskatoon, Edmonton, **Jasper**, and Kamloops.

Connections and Train Stations
Changing trains allows one to continue to travel elsewhere in Canada or to go to the United States. Between Winnipeg and Jasper, by crossing the Prairies, travellers who disembark can continue their journey by bus or by car.

Air shuttles link Vancouver with **Vancouver Island**, where travellers can board the **Victoria-Courtenay Train** (*The Malahat*). From Vancouver, it is possible to reach Alaska by cruise ship or by car, crossing fjords and glaciers. To reach California, it's possible to take **Amtrak** trains or drive through the state of Washington.

After a night in Jasper, the **Jasper-Prince-Rupert Train** (*The Skeena*) offers the opportunity to visit northern British Columbia, a truly spectacular region. From Winnipeg, it's possible to visit northern Manitoba onboard the **Winnipeg-Churchill Train** (*The Hudson Bay*).

In Toronto, there is direct access to southern Quebec and Ontario via numerous trains.

Schedule, rates and reservations
The Canadian departs Toronto and Vancouver three days a week. The days vary throughout the year. Check the website (www.viarail.ca) for departure dates.

Choice of classes
Comfort Class (Economy) offers a trip

with all the modern conveniences at a good price.

Silver and Blue Class, first class sleeper cars, offers top of the line accommodations including all meals, a comfortable bed, shower access and a lounge in the Park Car.

Single Rooms
A single room is suitable for one person and includes:
- a berth that changes into a sofa
- a small storage space for luggage
- a window with a shade
- a private washroom
- a sink above the toilet, with a wall-mounted mirror
- access to a shower near the room
- towels and a toiletry kit
- the door can only be locked from the inside (no individual keys)
- Other conveniences: a fan, a shoe rack, air conditioning, drinking water, paper and towels, pillows, sheets and blankets, 110v outlet.

Double Room
This room has upper and lower berths, is comfortable for two people and includes:
- during the day: two removable chairs
- at night: an upper and a lower berth replace the removable chairs
- private washroom accessible from the room
- a small storage space for luggage (approximately one suitcase and one travelling bag)
- a large window with a shade
- a mirror above the sink with an electrical outlet
- access to a shower near the room
- towels and a toiletry kit
- individual control of the fan, heating, and air conditioning
- the door can only be locked from the inside (no individual keys)
- Other conveniences: a small closet, drinking water, paper and towels, pillows, sheets and blankets

Meals
Breakfast, lunch, and dinner, too, all prepared on board by the chef, are included in the ticket price. Snacks, cocktails and coffee are served as well. In Toronto, Jasper, and Vancouver, passengers are welcomed aboard with hot hors d'oeuvres and sparkling wine.

Carry-on luggage
Each passenger is permitted a maximum of two carry-on bags.
The maximum dimension of each piece of carry-on luggage is 66 x 46 x 34 cm (26 x 18 x 9 in). The maximum weight for each piece of carry-on luggage is 23 kg (50 lb).

Smoking
This is a non-smoking train. It is possible to smoke when stopped in the stations at Capreol, Hornepayne, Sioux Lookout, Winnipeg, Saskatoon, Edmonton, Jasper and Kamloops.

Special Stops for the Adventurous
Between Capreol and Winnipeg, you can get off the train at the exact location you wish, even if no stop is planned. All you need to do is request a **special stop**. This service was established especially for lovers of the **great outdoors** who wish to disembark right in the forest.

Bicycles and Canoes
You can transport your bicycle or your canoe on certain trains.

USEFUL ADDRESSES
Toronto Landmark Hotel
The Fairmont Royal York
100 Front Street W
Toronto, Ontario
Canada M5J 1E3
Phone: (416) 368-2511
Fax: (416) 368-9040
Email: royalyorkhotel@fairmont.com

Mid-journey in Winnipeg, a historic spot to have a drink during a stopover
The Fort Garry Hotel
222 Broadway
Winnipeg, Manitoba
Canada R3C 0R3
Phone: (204) 942-8251
Fax: (204) 956-2351
Email: ftgarry@fortgarryhotel.com
Internet: www.fortgarryhotel.com

Acknowledgments

The authors' trip was organized by the Canadian Office of Tourism (c/o the Canadian Embassy, 35 Avenue Montaigne, 75008, Paris), following an invitation from VIA Rail, the company that runs *The Canadian.*
Special thanks go to Anne Zobenbuhler.

This book has been supported by the French Ministry of Foreign and European Affairs, as part of the translation grant program.

Olivier Barrot : Journalist, host of the daily France 3 and TV 5 program "Un livre un jour" since 1991, co-founder and editorial director of SENSO, "the magazine of pleasure and the senses." He teaches in Paris (Sciences Po), New York (NYU) and Montreal; and he writes books (theatre, travel, cinema...).

Alain Bouldouyre : A skilled artist who's passionate about travel, he has been around the world several times. He has also published a number of illustrated travel logs. He shares with his accomplice, Olivier Barrot, a taste for new and different places.

Together, they've written *Lettres à l'inconnue* and *Voyages au pays des salles obscures*, as well as many reports for SENSO. Alain Bouldouyre illustrated *Decalage horaire* and *Mon Angleterre* (Gallimard, "Folio") by Olivier Barrot.